Praying To Get Results

By Kenneth E. Hagin

Second Edition
Eighth Printing 1987

ISBN 0-89276-013-3

In the U.S. write:
Kenneth Hagin Ministries
P.O. Box 50126
Tulsa, OK 74150-0126

In Canada write:
Kenneth Hagin Ministries
P.O. Box 335
Islington (Toronto), Ontario
Canada, M9A 4X3

Contents

Chapter 1
Follow the Rules To Get Results

Praying always with all prayer and supplication in the Spirit . . . .

— Ephesians 6:18

There are different kinds of prayer, just as there are different games in sports, each with its own set of rules. Rules that apply to baseball do not apply to football. If you tried to use the same rules, you would get confused.

Similarly, there are rules or spiritual laws that govern certain kinds of prayer, but do not apply to other kinds of prayer. Sometimes we make a mistake by lumping together all kinds of prayers. Then we don't see the desired results.

As we look in God's Word to discover the kind of prayer that gets results, notice again our text, Ephesians 6:18. Moffatt's translation reads, "Praying. . .with all manner of prayer." Still another translation says, "Praying with all kinds of prayer."

For example, some people think every prayer should end with the words, "If it be thy will." They say this is the way Jesus prayed. But Jesus did not pray this way every time. When Jesus prayed at Lazarus' tomb, He didn't pray, "If it be thy will." He said, *"Father, I thank thee that thou hast heard me"* (John 11:41). He then commanded Lazarus to come forth, and Lazarus came forth.

This prayer was one to change circumstances. When you pray for something or to change circumstances, never pray "if." If you do, you're using the wrong rule and it won't work.

The only kind of prayer in which Jesus included an "if" was a prayer of consecration and dedication. In the Garden of Gethsemane He prayed, *"Father, if thou be willing, remove this cup from me: nevertheless not my will, but thine, be done"* (Luke 22:42). Jesus wasn't praying to change something. He was praying a prayer of consecration and dedication. And in this prayer, we should put an "if" because we want to be ready to do what Jesus wants us to do.

When it comes to believing God for something, we should not pray, "If it be thy will." We already have God's promise in His Word. It *is* His will that our needs be met. We read in Mark 11:24, *"What things soever ye desire, when ye pray, believe that ye receive them, and ye shall have them."* We should realize it is God's will that *all* our needs be met — spiritual, physical, and material.

Although we don't live under the Old Covenant, we can better understand the nature of God by studying the Old Testament. There we find that God promised His people more than spiritual blessings. He also promised they would prosper financially and materially. He promised He would take sickness away from them, and the number of their days He would fulfill (Exod. 23:25,26).

In Psalm 105:37 we read that when the Israelites were delivered from Egypt, there was not a feeble one among them — although there were some two million people!

God is interested in everything that touches our lives, and He has made provision for us. He promised the Old Testament saints if they would keep His commandments, they would eat the good of the land. This implies we are to prosper materially. The New Testament essentially says the same thing: *"Beloved, I wish above all things that thou mayest prosper and be in health, even as thy soul prospereth"* (3 John 1:2).

Jesus said He would give good gifts to His children because He is concerned about us. He is talking about the desires of our hearts, and He tells us how to get them. Let's go according to the rules!

The Scripture that says, *"What things soever ye desire,*

when ye pray, believe that ye receive them, and ye shall have them" (Mark 11:24) is talking about the prayer of faith. This primarily is an individual situation. It pertains to *your* desires. It is you praying; not someone else praying with you. It's not someone else agreeing with you. When *you* pray, *you* believe that *you* receive. If you'll do that, you'll have *"what things soever ye desire."* You'll get results!

I can make this work for myself, but I can't always make it work for you. Your will is involved. *One person's unbelief can nullify another person's prayer of faith.* Baby Christians usually can be carried on a mature Christian's faith, but after a certain period of time God expects them to develop their own prayer life and their own faith.

I've seen this demonstrated many times during my years in the field ministry. In those church meetings, I would teach mainly on faith and healing. Toward the end of the meetings, we would allow time for questions and answers. One question asked repeatedly was: "Why is it when I first got saved, I got my healing every time I was prayed for, but now I don't ever get healed?"

I would answer by saying that new Christians are like babies. No one is born a full-grown Christian. God wants us to grow and to mature. We feel pity for those who are physically deformed and who never have developed fully. We ought to have the same compassion for those who do not grow spiritually.

When you were first saved, you were a baby. Naturally, the pastor could carry you on his faith. There were Christians praying for you who would carry you, and their faith would work for you. But after a while, God knew that you had had the opportunity to grow, whether you grew or not. He said, "It's time to put that big baby down and let him walk." We really had a cry baby on our hands then. A lot of people still would rather be carried.

As a pastor, I noticed there were people who would get healed primarily on my faith. It was the easiest thing in the world for new converts or people who were babies on the subject of divine healing to get healed. *Those who had been Christians the longest were the hardest ones to get healed.*

After World War II, there was a revival of divine healing in America. It began about 1947 and lasted 10 years. I talked to various evangelists who were in the healing ministry, and every one of them said the same thing: You never would get people healed until you got past the Full Gospel Christians in the prayer line!

About six weeks after a meeting conducted by a leading evangelist in the early 1950s, a survey was sent to several thousand persons asking two questions: Did you receive healing when this man laid hands on you and prayed? Are you still healed?

Approximately 6,000 cards were returned, and out of that number only 3 percent of the Full Gospel people said they got healed. But 70 percent of the denominational people were healed, and 70 percent said they still had their healing six weeks later.

What made the difference? *God expected more from those who had been taught.* God expects people who know the full Gospel to operate their own faith. Yet many times they want to remain babies.

In one church my wife and I pastored, we had a healing service every Saturday night. One of our members was a woman who had arthritis. Her body was stiff as a board. If you took her out of the wheelchair and stood her on the floor, it would look like she was sitting down; her body was that stiff.

Although she was confined to a wheelchair, she was able to cook her meals and do her housework. If she caught the flu or had any minor ailment, we could pray for her, and she would get healed.

Finally, one day we went to her house to pray, *determined* to see her delivered from that wheelchair. As we prayed, the power of God came on her and lifted her out of that chair — into the air — out in front of the chair!

"Oh, oh, oh" she began to say as she reached back with those little, crippled hands and pulled that chair up under her. She fell down in the chair.

I pointed my finger at her and said, "Sister, you don't have an ounce of faith, do you?" (She was saved and baptized with the Holy Spirit, but I meant she didn't have faith for her healing.)

Without thinking, she blurted out, "No, Brother Hagin, I don't! I don't believe I'll ever be healed. I'll go to my grave from this chair." She said it, and she did it.

We weren't to blame. We had prayed the healing power of God down on that woman. If she had *believed* and *received* that power, it would have loosed her and healed every joint in her body. That's the reason we have seminars and other meetings — to teach people so they can grow in faith.

Years ago, I learned that my sister had cancer. I went to the Lord in prayer on her behalf. I battled with the devil for her life. The Lord told me she would live and not die. The cancer was curtailed, and she had no more symptoms. Five years passed, and then she developed an entirely different form of cancer in another part of her body. There was no relation to the first cancer; it was of a different type.

My sister got down to 79 pounds. The Lord kept telling me that she was going to die. I kept asking the Lord why I couldn't change the outcome. He told me she had had five years in which she could have studied the Word and built up her faith (she was saved), but she hadn't done it. He told me she was going to die, and she did. This is a sad example, but it's so true.

If the church is growing, there will continue to be new babies in Christ. But if everybody in the church stayed babies, who would care for these new ones? An evangelist primarily is interested in winning the lost. But if everyone were an evangelist, the people who get saved always would be babies. God saw these babies needed a shepherd and He set pastors in the church. He wanted the sheep to be fed. He also put teachers in the church to help people grow in faith and the knowledge of the Word.

My son, who is more than 40 years old, is an ordained minister. For the first 15 years of his life, I carried him on my faith and did his praying for him. He always received his healing. But when Ken was 15 years old, He got a severe ear infection. His ear was really hurting him and he wanted to go to the doctor. The doctor said he had an incurable fungus condition in one ear which he probably got from swimming.

Ken kept having to go back to the doctor to have his ear cleaned. The doctor said he probably would lose his hearing in that ear, and it would cause him trouble all his life.

The Lord told me that He expected my boy to walk in the light of what he knew because he knew the way. The Lord said my praying wouldn't work for him anymore.

At Christmas time, I had to take Ken back to the doctor to have the fungus cleaned out of his ear again. The doctors said he couldn't go swimming anymore because the more he was around water, the faster the fungus would grow. I told my son what the Lord had told me. I told him he would have to believe God for himself.

Ken looked at me, still wanting to use my faith for his healing. I told him that while I would kneel with him when he prayed, I wasn't going to pray at all; he had to pray for himself. He prayed and got his healing. Years have passed and the fungus never reappeared.

If people follow their natural inclinations, they want to remain babies and let someone else carry them. But you can pray the prayer of faith for yourself; quit saying you can't.

Everywhere it says "you" in the following Scripture, insert your name: *"Therefore, I say unto YOU, what things soever YOU desire, when YOU pray, believe that YOU receive them, and YOU shall have them"* (Mark 11:24).

That's what my son did when he prayed. When we got up off our knees, he didn't have any evidence of healing. But when I asked him if he were healed, he said, "Yes!" He said he was healed because the Bible said so.

You have to profess and believe God even though the things you desire in prayer haven't manifested yet. You have to stand your ground. If someone questions you, say you believe God heard you. Tell them you don't care what the devil says, because you believe God and His Word.

Then you'll see results!

Chapter 2
Exchange Petition for Praise

As they ministered to the Lord, and fasted,
the Holy Ghost said, Separate me Barnabas and
Saul for the work whereunto I have called them.
— Acts 13:2

Often it seems the only kind of prayer we are familiar with is the petition prayer. We're always petitioning (or asking) God to do something, and of course that's scriptural. But in the Scripture quoted above, those Christians were not petitioning God to do anything. They *"ministered to the Lord, and fasted . . . ."*

Most of our church services are designed so we come together and minister to one another. We sing, but in very few songs do we minister to the Lord. Instead, we minister to one another. We have special singing, but still we're not ministering to the Lord; we're ministering to one another.

When we pray, our praying is primarily a petition. We're petitioning the Lord to move in our midst, to manifest Himself among us, to meet our needs. When the minister speaks, he's not ministering to the Lord; he's ministering to the congregation. And when the service is over, if we have a time of waiting on God, usually these prayers are still petitions.

We know God is concerned about us and wants to meet our needs. Jesus said our heavenly Father knows what we need, and we should ask Him to supply these needs. But, too much of the time we're like the little boy who said, "My name's Jimmy, and I'll take all you'll gimme!"

We need times of waiting on God and ministering to the Lord; times when we're not asking for anything — not petitioning — but ministering to Him. Perhaps we are already taking time for this in our individual prayer lives,

8

but we need this kind of prayer as a group or a church. God can move in this kind of atmosphere. As they ministered to the Lord, and fasted, our text says, the Holy Ghost manifested Himself.

God made man to fellowship with Him. He is our Father, because we are born of God. I'm sure of this: There are no earthly parents who enjoy the fellowship of their children more than God enjoys the fellowship of His children.

In one meeting I held, I said to the people after the sixth week, "Let's have some different kinds of services. I want us to come to minister to the Lord. I may read a little bit of Scripture, or make a few comments, but I'm not going to preach or teach a lot. We're not going to come to petition God; we're going to wait on the Lord and minister to Him.

"I don't want us to come and wait 10 minutes. I want us to come with the thought that we're going to wait at least one hour. We'll minister to the Lord — tell Him how much we love Him and thank Him for His goodness and mercy."

The people came and praised the Lord. I found they wanted to wait on God. In that kind of atmosphere, God ministered to us in very unusual ways. Although that was years ago, there still are things happening today as a result of what the Lord did in those services.

I'm sure of this: *We miss a lot of what God has for us because we don't take time to get into an attitude of worship and minister to the Lord.*

A Bible example of this is found in the 16th chapter of Acts. Paul and Silas were arrested in Philippi, where they had gone to preach the Gospel. They were beaten with many stripes and cast into prison. The jailer was charged to keep them safely, *"Who, having received such a charge, thrust them into the inner prison, and made their feet fast in the stock"* (v. 24).

Notice particularly the 25th verse, *"And at midnight Paul and Silas prayed, and sang praises unto God: and the prisoners heard them."*

They certainly couldn't have been singing some of the songs we sing, because many of our songs don't praise God. Too often our songs are more of a complaint than a praise. The songs seem to have the "poor old me" attitude — we're wandering through life destitute, downtrodden, and in dark valleys. Too much of the time the songs are about *us* — what we're doing and how rough life is. If we do sing anything about heaven, it's about when we all get there. That still doesn't give God any praise.

But Paul and Silas sang praises to God. Notice, too, the prisoners heard them. They weren't quiet about this!

If Paul and Silas had been like a lot of people today, instead of praying and singing praises at midnight, they would've been griping and complaining. And the Scripture might have read something like this: About midnight Paul and Silas griped and complained and Silas nudged Paul and said, "Paul, are you still there?"

It's very dark, so Paul says, "Where else could I be?"

Silas would have said, "You know, Paul, you really missed God, didn't you?"

While Paul is trying to figure out where he missed it, Silas says, "I'll tell you one thing, when I was serving the devil, I never got thrown in jail. I don't know why God let this happen to us. Why, if I ever get out of here — and I doubt I will — I'll be ashamed to go home, because they'll call me an old jailbird. I tell you, Paul, I got hooked up with the wrong fellow — that's all there is to it."

"Yeah — we missed it somewhere," Paul says. "And I tell you, my poor back is really hurting me bad. You know, I really thought God was speaking to me in that vision, but if God were in it, we'd have been a success."

During the 12 years I pastored, I heard members of my church say similar things. "I never had it this rough when I was serving the devil," some would say when a trial came their way. How do you help people like that?

Well, I would smile and say, "God will forgive you of that, too, if you'll repent."

Paul and Silas really were in trouble, weren't they? They were thrust into the inner prison. They had been whipped with many stripes until their backs were bleeding. Their feet were in stocks. I'm sure they were in great physical pain.

It was a dark hour for them, but although Paul and Silas were in jail, they didn't let the jail get in them. That's the reason a lot of people are defeated.

Everyone has trouble of one kind or another. We've all been lashed by the storms of life. But our attitude — how we look at a situation and how we accept it — makes the difference in how we come out, or whether we get out at all.

In our midnight hour, when we don't understand why things have happened, even though we've tried our best, let us look at Paul and Silas. After all, they didn't go to Philippi on a pleasure trip. They were there to do the Lord's work. *They were not out of the will of God.*

Sometimes when things don't go right, people think, "I must be out of the will of God." Or they ask, "What awful sin have I committed to cause God to send this on me?" God didn't send the trouble; the devil did. It wasn't God who whipped Paul and Silas; it was ungodly men. God didn't stir up those ungodly fellows; it was the devil.

In spite of persecution, adversity, and depressing surroundings, *"At midnight Paul and Silas prayed, and sang praises unto God, and the prisoners heard them."* They weren't quiet about it! They were praising God at midnight right out loud in jail.

A characteristic of the early disciples was their continual praises to God. We read in Luke 24:50-53:

> **LUKE 24:50-53**
> 50 And he led them out as far as to Bethany, and he lifted
> up his hands, and blessed them.
> 51 And it came to pass, while he blessed them, he was
> parted from them, and carried up into heaven.
> 52 And they worshipped him, and returned to Jerusalem
> with great joy:
> 53 And were continually in the temple, praising and bless-
> ing God.

Then notice the second chapter of Acts, verses 46 and 47:

> **ACTS 2:46,47**
> 46 And they, continuing daily with one accord in the temple,
> and breaking bread from house to house, did eat with glad-
> ness and singleness of heart,
> 47 Praising God, and having favour with all the people.
> And the Lord added to the church daily such as should be
> saved.

Notice the expression, *"with gladness and singleness
of heart, praising God."* One reason the ministry of the
early Christians was so effective was their continual
gladness of heart and praising God.

Worship and praise to God were a part of the daily lives
of the early Christians. It wasn't something they did occasionally. Too many times today we see people who pray
through about once every six months. You'd have to write
of them that they praised God "occasionally" or perhaps
"semi-annually" rather than "daily" or "continually," as
did the New Testament believers.

The late Smith Wigglesworth once said, "First thing
every morning, when I get out of bed, I jump out. I don't
just drag out, but I jump out! And when my feet hit the
floor I say, 'Praise the Lord!' And I praise God every
morning." That's a good way to start the day!

When Paul and Silas were thrown in jail at Philippi,
it was only natural they should pray and sing praises to

God. Not only did the prisoners hear them, but God heard them. Suddenly there was such a great earthquake that the foundations of the prison shook! All the doors sprung open. Everyone's bonds were loosed. *Deliverance came while they were praising God!*

An Old Testament counterpart is found in Second Chronicles 20, when Jehoshaphat went out against the enemy. Three armies — the Ammonites, the Moabites, and the inhabitants of Mount Seir — had banded together against Jehoshaphat. He didn't have the manpower to stand against them, so he called a prayer meeting. The people fasted and prayed.

The Spirit of God moved upon a young man in the congregation, and he stood and prophesied. The Lord told them not to fear. He told them where the enemy was and said to go against them because the battle was the Lord's.

The next morning they marched against the enemy, and the Bible says they put the praisers up front. Picture these men going against three armies of trained soldiers who had swords, javelins, and spears. Right up front to lead the parade of God's army were the praisers. They weren't led by a man with a sword or a spear. *They were led by men singing and praising the Lord.*

They ministered to the Lord. As they marched along, they shouted, *"Praise the Lord; for His mercy endureth for ever"* (2 Chron. 20:21).

We see in the next verse what happened as a result: *"And when they began to sing and to praise, the Lord set ambushments against the children of Ammon, Moab, and mount Seir, which were come against Judah; and they were smitten."*

When they began to sing and praise, God did something for His people. They saw a manifestation of His power. They didn't have to draw a sword or throw a javelin. The enemy ran off and left all their goods. There was so much spoil it took three days to gather it up and carry it home!

Paul and Silas had their feet in stocks. Their backs were bleeding. From the natural standpoint, they had every reason to be downcast. But at midnight, as they ministered to God, there came a manifestation of God's power.

There are many today who have been praying and petitioning God to move in their behalf. If they would quit praying and begin praising, God would give them so much they couldn't carry it all home at one time!

We need to have praise services where we gather to praise God and to minister to the Lord — not to minister to one another — not to brag on one another — not to tell what I have and you don't — or what I'm trying to get.

We need services where we minister to the Lord and sing praises to Him. Then we would see mighty manifestations of God's presence in our day.

Chapter 3
You Don't Have To Worry

Be careful for nothing; but in every thing by prayer and supplication with thanksgiving let your requests be made known unto God.

— Philippians 4:6

Casting all your care upon him; for he careth for you.

— 1 Peter 5:7

Casting the whole of your care — all your anxieties, all your worries, all your concerns, once and for all — on Him; for He cares for you affectionately, and cares about you watchfully.

— 1 Peter 5:7 *(AMPLIFIED)*

One evening after a service, a woman came to me and said, "I want you to agree with me in prayer about something. The burdens of life — the cares, the worries of life — are just so heavy I can't bear them."

She began to cry. With sincerity she said, "I want you to pray God will either give me grace to bear these burdens or else take about half of them away. I can carry about half of them — I just can't carry all of them."

"Dear Sister," I replied, "we don't have to pray about that — we've already heard from heaven. God's Word is our message from heaven. His Word couldn't be more sure if an angel suddenly came down here and wrote with his finger on a granite block: GOD'S WORD IS ETERNAL."

She looked startled.

I opened my Bible to First Peter 5:7 and asked her to read out loud. She read, *"Casting all your care upon him; for he careth for you."*

Then I said, "I can't pray God would give you grace

15

to bear your cares and worries. He doesn't want you to bear them. And I can't pray God would take away half of them, because He doesn't want you to carry even half of them. He wants you to cast *all* of them on Him."

"I can't do it!" she said.

I said, "Sister, God is not telling you to do something you can't do. He would be an unjust God to do that. You've been praying about this for years and have never gotten an answer. That's not the way to solve this problem. You solve this by doing what God said to do."

"Yeah," she replied, *"but you don't know what I've got to worry about!"*

"But God does," I said. "He knows and understands. And He said to cast all your cares upon Him."

It seemed to me a person would be glad to find that verse in the Bible and would be thrilled to act upon it. But she turned, walked away, and said, "I couldn't give up worrying."

Some people are content in the knowledge that God knows and understands their problems. But still they hold on to their cares, so they don't get deliverance. It's not enough that God cares and understands. We must go on and do what He said to do — cast all of our cares on Him, for He cares for us. This is the prayer of commitment, of casting or rolling our cares and burdens on Him.

Psalm 37:5 says, *"Commit thy way unto the Lord; trust also in him; and he shall bring it to pass."*

Jesus had this to say:

MATTHEW 6:25-27
25 Take no thought for your life, what ye shall eat, or what ye shall drink; nor yet for your body, what ye shall put on. Is not the life more than meat, and the body than raiment? 26 Behold the fowls of the air: for they sow not, neither do they reap, nor gather into barns; yet your heavenly Father feedeth them. Are ye not much better than they?

**27 Which of you by taking thought can add one cubit unto
his stature?**

Jesus is asking which of you by worrying is going to
change anything. Luke records, *"Therefore, I say unto you,
Take no thought for your life...."* (Luke 12:22).

Paul said in Philippians 4:6, *"Be careful for
nothing...." The Amplified Bible* reads, "Do not fret or
have any anxiety about anything...." Too many times
people want to pray and get God to do something about
their anxieties. But God tells *you* to do something about
them. He said, *"Be careful for nothing."* Or, "Don't *you*
fret or have anxiety about anything."

As long as you do not take this first step — as long
as you fret and have anxiety — you are nullifying the effects
of your prayer. You haven't cast your burden on the Lord.
You still have it. And if you have it, God doesn't.

Casting all your care on Him isn't something you do
every day. It's a once-and-for-all proposition. This puts
your situation in His hands. The Lord could do a lot for
us, but often we don't let Him because we don't follow His
rules that govern the operation of prayer. We don't do
what He tells us to do. Then we wonder why things don't
work out.

If you cast your burden on the Lord, He has it. You
don't. You cannot go around talking about your worries
anymore. *A lot of people don't want to get rid of their worries.* They claim they do, but they really don't. If they got
rid of them, they wouldn't have any reason for people to
sympathize with them. They wouldn't have anything to
talk about. They would have to cease conversation entirely.

Years ago, when I was on the bed of sickness, this was
the first thing God began to deal with me about. I had
to quit worrying before I could receive healing for my body.
This is the reason a lot of people are not healed. Sometimes
worry is what is keeping them sick. Any disappearance

of the symptoms would only be temporary, because the cause of the sickness is still there.

You may think a 15-year-old boy couldn't worry. But children are replicas of their parents, and my grandmother and mother were *world-champion worriers*. As a child, I knew they were always worrying. I had a heart condition, and I couldn't go out to run and play like other children. I had to stay in with my mother and grandmother. Hearing them complain and worry, I learned to worry at a very early age.

While on the bed of sickness, I got saved, and I promised God I would never doubt anything I read in His Word. I further said, "As I read the Word and better understand it, I promise to put it into practice."

I read the 26th verse in Matthew 6, *"Take no thought for your life...."* The Bible I was reading had a footnote that told me the Greek read, "Do not be anxious about tomorrow." Another reference said, "Do not worry, do not be filled with anxiety." I was full of anxiety, worry, and fear. Not only was I nearly dead, but also I was about to worry myself the rest of the way to my grave!

My conscience bothered me because I was not practicing the Word. As the Lord dealt with me, the words seemed to leap from the pages of the Bible. Yet I didn't think I could live without worrying — without being anxious — so I closed my Bible. When I did, I got in darkness. I opened the Word again and tried to read, bypassing that Scripture.

Until then, everything I'd read had been all light and blessing, but now it was all dark and fuzzy to me. You're not going to get more light (or understanding) until you walk in the light you already have. Don't be concerned about the things you don't understand in God's Word; make sure you practice what you do know. The rest will take care of itself.

I read on. I even studied about the Antichrist. (That certainly was not what was bothering me.) But I felt guilty because I was not practicing the Word. Finally, I made a commitment to God.

I said, "Lord, forgive me for worrying and for being full of anxiety. Forgive me for fretting and for being discouraged. Forgive me for having the blues and feeling sorry for myself. Forgive me for having a 'poor old me' attitude. I know You'll forgive me, because You said You would if I would confess it. From this day on, because You've forgiven me, I promise I'll never worry again. I'll never be filled with anxiety again. I'll never be blue again. I'll never fret again. I'll never be discouraged again."

Many years have passed since I made that commitment. Although I'll confess I've been sorely tempted, just like you have, I have not worried. I haven't been filled with anxiety at any time or become overly anxious. I haven't had the blues in all these years! *God's Word works.* I wouldn't encourage you to do anything I wouldn't do, or haven't done.

When I was 21 years old, I was pastor of a church which was 23 years old. There were people in that church who had had the baptism of the Holy Spirit two years longer than I had lived. You can understand why I would feel insufficient. The church had problems, and I knew something should be said, but I didn't know what to say. I knew if I said anything, I would say the wrong thing.

I prayed, "Lord, there are problems here. I don't know what to do. I feel so inadequate." I could sense the Spirit of God reminding me of the Scripture, *"Casting all your cares upon him; for he careth for you"* (1 Peter 5:7).

I said, "Lord, I know I have responsibilities as pastor, but I'm going to turn this over to You. I'm not going to worry. I'm going to preach the Word and leave everything else to You."

My burden lifted and I went singing on my way to church. God met us and marvelous things happened.

The ministers in our area had a fellowship meeting on the first Monday of every month. The preachers talked about their burdens, cares, responsibilities, and anxieties. Often they would ask me, "How goes the battle?" (They were all in a battle, but I didn't have any battle. I had the victory! Men in battle haven't won the victory yet. The battle is the Lord's; the victory is ours.)

Here were these preachers with long faces talking about their burdens, cares, and problems in their churches. One of them said to me later, "Your faith condemned us when you'd wave your hand and say, 'Men, I don't have a care! Things couldn't be better!' "

Some would shake their heads and say, "The poor boy — he doesn't have enough sense to worry." The truth is, *I had too much sense — too much Bible sense — to worry!* If I had cast my cares on the Lord, then I didn't have them. He did. I didn't say no cares existed. I said, "I don't have a care."

One pastor would say, "He's lying. I'm his neighboring pastor, and I know him better than the rest of you. I know about the problems in his church."

But I'd breeze by and say, "Men, I don't have a care!" I didn't. I had cast them on the Lord once and for all. *You can, too!*

Chapter 4
United Prayer Gets Results

> *And being let go, THEY WENT TO THEIR OWN COMPANY, and reported all that the chief priests and elders had said unto them.*
>
> *And when they heard that, they lifted up their voice to God with one accord, and said, Lord, thou art God, which has made heaven, and earth, and the sea, and all that in them is . . . .*
>
> *Grant unto thy servants, that with all boldness they may speak thy word,*
>
> *By stretching forth thine hand to heal; and that signs and wonders may be done by the name of thy holy child Jesus.*
>
> — Acts 4:23,24,29,30

It's good to be among friends when you're in trouble. It's good to be with people who know how to pray. Peter and John found this to be true.

One day, as Peter and John passed through the Gate Beautiful on their way to the Temple, they saw a man who sat there daily to beg alms. Peter told the man, *"Look on us."* The beggar looked up, expecting to receive some coins.

Peter said, *"Silver and gold have I none; but such as I have give I thee: In the name of Jesus Christ of Nazareth rise up and walk"* (Acts 3:6).

Peter took the beggar by the hand and lifted him up. The man began to walk and went into the Temple *"walking and leaping, and praising God."* Peter and John were arrested, threatened, and commanded to preach and teach no more in the Name of Jesus.

We read in Acts 4:23-30 what happened when they were released. *"And being let go, they went to their own company, and reported all that the chief priests and elders had said unto them . . . ."*

It was good to be among friends who knew how to pray!

If this company of believers had been like some people in churches today, they would have appointed a committee to make some kind of deal whereby they could get along together. After all, these chief priests and elders were religious people, too. Although they didn't accept Jesus as Messiah, they believed in the same God, in prayer, and in going to the Temple.

But this company of believers didn't appoint any committee; they didn't make any deals. They *"lifted up their voice to God with one accord." There's power in united prayer.*

Coming from different church backgrounds, sometimes we're used to doing things a certain way. Sometimes we think the way we've always done them is the way they *ought* to be done. I was raised in a Southern Baptist church and was not accustomed to hearing people pray out loud in united prayer. Usually in our church, an individual led in prayer, but we never lifted our voices as a congregation.

My grandmother, however, had been saved many years before in an old-fashioned Methodist campmeeting, so she was accustomed to hearing people pray out loud.

Later, when some Full Gospel people came to our town and put up a tent, my grandmother went to their meetings. She told me I should go, too. I already had been saved and healed, although I never had heard the name "Full Gospel" before.

I stopped by one night and stood outside the tent listening to the message. The next week I went by and went inside the tent for the whole service. After the minister had preached, he came back through the crowd, shaking hands with people and asking if they were Christians. Practically everyone he talked to went to the altar. He asked me if I were a Christian. I told him I was a minister. He told me to go to the altar and pray because it wouldn't hurt me. Then he went on.

We didn't do things that way in our church. For a moment, I felt a bit insulted. I never had heard of prayer hurting anybody, so I went down and prayed. But I was bothered because they did all their praying out loud and I did mine quietly.

A church was built from this revival, and I went to the services because they stimulated my faith. But when I would go down to the altar to pray, I would move far away from the others. One time I ventured to tell them God wasn't hard of hearing. They replied He wasn't nervous, either!

As I got to thinking, I remembered that these people knew about divine healing and my church didn't. And they were right about divine healing. They might know some other things I didn't know.

I decided to read through the Book of Acts and underline with red pencil everywhere two or more prayed in a group. I was going to see how they did it back then.

As I read through Acts underlining these Scriptures, I couldn't find a single place where there was a group and one person was called on to lead in prayer. I also couldn't find sentence prayers or anything like that. I found the Bible said they lifted their voices. They all prayed at once, and they all prayed out loud!

The next time I went to the Full Gospel services, I got right in the middle of them when they prayed.

Chapter 5
Paul at Prayer

And this I pray, that your love may abound yet
more and more in knowledge and in all judgment.
— Philippians 1:9

Many times when praying for Christians we say, "God bless Sister So-and-so" and "God bless Brother So-and-so," yet we don't find where Paul ever prayed that way. That kind of praying really doesn't do much good; it only salves our conscience and makes us feel we've prayed.

Paul was specific when he said, *"I pray, that your love may abound more and more."* That's a good way to pray for Christians, isn't it? Paul is praying for believers.

Notice Colossians 1:9:

> **COLOSSIANS 1:9**
> 9 For this cause we also, since the day we heard it, do not cease to pray for you, and to desire that ye might be filled with the knowledge of his will in all wisdom and spiritual understanding.

This is Paul's prayer for the Church at Colosse. If you are filled with the knowledge of His Will, then you're going to know what all these blessings are with which the Father has blessed you.

In Ephesians 1:3, Paul prayed:

> **EPHESIANS 1:3**
> 3 Blessed be the God and Father of our Lord Jesus Christ, who hath blessed us with all spiritual blessings in heavenly places in Christ.

That means He already has provided everything we need — all the blessings we will ever need. *They are all wrapped up in Jesus.*

To pray, "God bless So-and-so" would cause God to say, "I can't answer that prayer. I've already done that,

but they don't know it." Instead of Paul's saying, "God
bless them," he said, *"[My] desire [is] that ye might be filled
with the knowledge of his will in all wisdom and spiritual
understanding."* That would be a good way to pray for
Christians. That's what most Christians need, isn't it?

Paul wrote this prayer under the inspiration of the Holy
Spirit. Since it's Spirit given, it would be a good prayer
for you to pray for yourself. You can say, "Lord, I'm going
to pray this prayer for myself. It's my desire and prayer
that I might be filled with the knowledge of your will in
all wisdom and spiritual understanding."

I think these prayers Paul prayed for the Christian
Church will give us insight on how to pray for other
believers as well.

For example, Paul wrote in Second Thessalonians 1:11:

2 THESSALONIANS 1:11
11 Wherefore also we pray always for you, that our God
would count you worthy of this calling, and fulfil all the
good pleasure of his goodness, and the work of faith with
power: that the name of our Lord Jesus Christ may be
glorified in you, and ye in him, according to the grace of
our God and the Lord Jesus Christ.

I particularly like where Paul said, *"fulfil all the good
pleasure of his goodness, and the work of faith with
power."* (That's what God wants fulfilled in us.) I also like
the phrase, *"that the Name of the Lord Jesus Christ may
be glorified in you."* Whoever thought of praying for a
whole church that the Name of the Lord Jesus Christ
might be glorified in them? Are you praying that way?
This is a clue for us. I'm convinced we need to be specific
in our praying one for another.

Paul was very specific and very definite in his praying. Let's look at more Scripture where Paul said something about prayer. Second Corinthians 1:11 isn't exactly

his prayer for the Corinthians, but Paul is asking their help in prayer: *"Ye also helping together by prayer for us . . . . "* Paul already had said in the 10th verse, concerning his difficulties, *"Who delivered us from so great a death, and doth deliver: in whom we trust that he will deliver us."* And then he said, *"Ye also helping together by prayer for us, that for the gift bestowed upon us by the means of many persons thanks may be given by many on our behalf"* (v. 11).

He is talking here about the prayer of the church "helping together." The church had prayed for him, hadn't they? The Bible says, *"The effectual fervent prayer of a righteous man availeth much"* (James 5:16). We are encouraged to pray one for another. When people are in trouble, or if their lives are in danger — like Paul's was — we need to remember to pray.

In Second Corinthians 9:14, Paul said, *"And by their prayer for you, which long after you for the exceeding grace of God in you."* Here he is talking about other people in his company who also had prayed for the Corinthians. They prayed one for another; they were concerned one for another.

We are selfish many times in our praying. Really, we should put others first in our prayer life. Most of the time, all we do is pray for ourselves and our own little group or family — our own needs.

We are much like the farmer who said, "God bless me and my wife, my son John and his wife, us four and no more." We wouldn't say it that way, but if you analyze it, that's about the extent of many of our prayers!

For an individual to grow spiritually, he's going to have to reach out and help others. You can't put yourself first. For a church to grow and develop, it's going to have to do the same thing.

In Philippians, Paul makes mention of praying for the

Church at Philippi, *"I thank my God upon every remembrance of you"* (Phil. 1:3). This is quite a statement, isn't it?

Do you remember what happened at Philippi? Do you remember when Paul first went down there? In a night vision, a man stood up and said, *"Come over to Macedonia, and help us"* (Acts 16:9). Paul had decided to go into Asia Minor, but said he was forbidden to go by the Spirit. So Paul and Silas went over into Macedonia, and thus the first time the Gospel was preached on the European continent was in Philippi. This is what happened:

> **ACTS 16:13,14**
> **13 And on the sabbath we went out of the city by a river side, where prayer was wont to be made; and we sat down, and spake unto the women which resorted thither.**
> **14 And a certain woman named Lydia, a seller of purple, of the city of Thyatira, which worshipped God, heard us: whose heart the Lord opened, that she attended unto the things which were spoken of Paul.**

Lydia was converted to Christianity and invited Paul and Silas to stay in her home. While in that city, Paul would often go into the synagogue and discuss the Scriptures.

On the streets of Philippi, a little maiden with a spirit of divination, or fortune-telling, would follow along behind Paul and Silas and say, *"These men are servants of the most high God, which shew unto us the way of salvation"* (Acts 16:17). She knew who they were because the evil spirit in her knew. (But who wants the devil testifying for him?)

Finally, one day Paul turned around on the street and cast the devil out of her — making it impossible for her to tell fortunes any more. Her masters became angry and had Paul and Silas arrested. They were stripped, beaten, and thrown in jail. At midnight they prayed and sang praises to God, as we studied earlier.

This Church at Philippi was born in persecution, yet Paul says, *"I thank my God upon every remembrance of you"* (Phil. 1:3). When you have the right perspective, you can thank God for every test. I always thank God for them. I thank God when I am in the midst of them, and I thank God when they're over; *not because they are over,* but because I had the *privilege* of proving Him faithful.

Believers should be full of joy and love, like a sponge is full of water. Then when the devil puts pressure on you, all that oozes out is joy and love instead of griping and complaining!

". . .Making request with joy, For your fellowship in the gospel from the first day until now" (Phil. 1:4,5). When Paul and Silas were in jail at Philippi, they prayed and sang praises to God. *Anyone can sing praises to God after he has been delivered; it doesn't take faith to do that.* But Paul and Silas sang praises to God at midnight while they were in the midst of trouble. That's the way it should be!

Paul says several things that give us a clue about how to pray for others and about our attitude in prayer. This is what he wrote to the Romans:

> **ROMANS 1:9-12**
> 9 For God is my witness, whom I serve with my spirit in the gospel of his Son, that without ceasing I make mention of you always in my prayers;
> 10 Making request, if by any means now at length I might have a prosperous journey by the will of God to come unto you.
> 11 For I long to see you, that I may impart unto you some spiritual gift, to the end ye may be established;
> 12 That is, that I may be comforted together with you by the mutual faith both of you and me.

From verse 9 we see that Paul never forgot to pray for the Romans. (It is so easy to forget, isn't it?) When he prayed for them, he mentioned one of his requests was that

"I might have a prosperous journey by the will of God to come unto you." He wanted to be made a blessing to them; he wanted to impart spiritual things to them.

Then again, we have Paul's prayers in Ephesians. These are the longest prayers Paul prayed; they are more detailed than prayers in his other letters.

EPHESIANS 1:16-23
16 [I] cease not to give thanks for you, making mention of you in my prayers,
17 That the God of our Lord Jesus Christ, the Father of glory, may give unto you the spirit of wisdom and revelation in the knowledge of him:
18 The eyes of your understanding being enlightened; that ye may know what is the hope of his calling, and what the riches of the glory of his inheritance in the saints,
19 And what is the exceeding greatness of his power to usward who believe, according to the working of his mighty power,
20 Which he wrought in Christ, when he raised him from the dead, and set him at his own right hand in the heavenly places,
21 Far above all principality, and power, and might, and dominion, and every name that is named, not only in this world, but also in that which is to come:
22 And hath put all things under his feet, and gave him to be the head over all things to the church,
23 Which is his body, the fulness of him that filleth all in all.

Paul prayed that the Ephesians might receive a revelation of the knowledge of God in their *hearts*; in other words, that the inner man might be enlightened.

One translation says, "The eyes of your heart, or your spirit . . . ." (Eph. 1:18). Paul didn't pray for their *mental* understanding, because we know it's beyond human (mental) comprehension to grasp the meaning of what Paul said here under the inspiration of the Holy Spirit. We know the Word means what it says, but we need to get the revelation of it in our hearts.

I made giant strides in my spiritual life when I began to pray this Ephesian prayer for myself. At my last pastorate in Texas, I shut myself up in my church during the winter of 1947-48 for hours and even days, never coming out.

I left my Bible open to this chapter on the altar, and nearly every time I went in, I got on my knees and prayed this prayer for myself.

I would say, "Now, Lord, Paul was inspired by the Spirit of God to pray this prayer, and he was inspired by the Spirit of God to write it. I am praying it for myself." Every place Paul said *your*, I would insert *I*. Where he said, "I pray that the eyes of *your* understanding . . . ." I would say, "I pray that the eyes of *my* understanding . . . ."

Then I would turn to the next prayer, in Ephesians 3:14-21, and I would pray for myself again. Since I would be there for hours at a time, I would pray those prayers every two or three hours — perhaps half a dozen times a day.

The Lord spoke to me one day while I was at the altar praying. He said, "I am going to take you on to revelations and visions." Immediately after that, revelations in line with the Word began to come. In fact, they came so fast I said to my wife, "What in the world have I been preaching the last 15 years?" I learned so much and got so much new knowledge from the Bible, praying these prayers on my knees before God, it seemed as if I didn't know anything before.

When the eyes of your understanding — your spirit — are enlightened, you can make more spiritual progress in a few days or weeks than you can in 15 years of studying the Bible and preaching. That doesn't mean we shouldn't study; I still study! But I'm saying these are good prayers to pray for yourself.